MW00597536

My
KAWAII
Journal

NAME ___Emilia___

ADDRESS _____

_____

CONTACT _____

_____

DAVID & CHARLES

www.davidandcharles.com

Key

Fill in the boxes with your own symbols for events and tasks, then use this as a key for your journal!

🐋	To-do
	Box-Sets
✎📦	Exam
🎈	Birthday
🎂	Party
Important	Important
✓	Done
⤳	Postponed
✗	Cancelled

Index

Future log

January

M	T	W	T	F	S	S

February

M	T	W	T	F	S	S

March

M	T	W	T	F	S	S

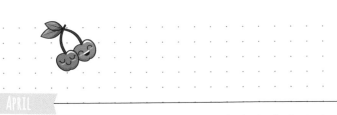

APRIL

M	T	W	T	F	S	S

MAY

M	T	W	T	F	S	S

JUNE

M	T	W	T	F	S	S

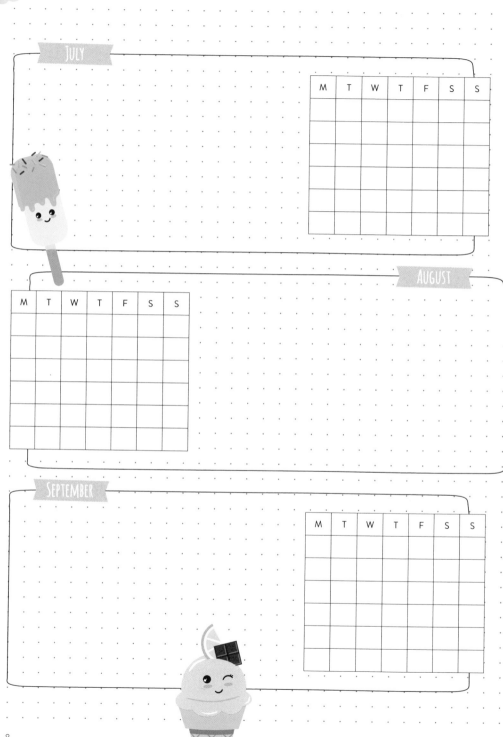

July

M	T	W	T	F	S	S

August

M	T	W	T	F	S	S

September

M	T	W	T	F	S	S

October

M	T	W	T	F	S	S

November

M	T	W	T	F	S	S

December

M	T	W	T	F	S	S

Weekly Schedule

TIME	MONDAY	TUESDAY	WEDNESDAY	THURSDAY	FRIDAY

TIME	MONDAY	TUESDAY	WEDNESDAY	THURSDAY	FRIDAY

Habit Tracker

My Sports Goal. ~~Streach~~ Study ~~Study~~ (e.g. 3 times per week)
My Learning Goal: ~~Study~~ Streach   My ..... Weekly ..... Goal: 5

Week	Sport	Learning	....
1.			
2.			
3.			
4.			
5.			
6.			
7.			
8.			
9.			
10.			
11.			
12.			
13.			
14.			
15.			
16.			
17.			
18.			
19.			
20.			
21.			
22.			

23.
24.
25.
26.
27.
28.
29.
30.
31.
32.
33.
34.
35.
36.
37.
38.
39.
40.
41.
42.
43.
44.
45.
46.
47.
48.
49.
50.
51.
52.
53.

My Teachers

Keep all the details of your teachers or professors in this handy section.

SUBJECT: ....

TEACHER: ....

EMAIL: ....

ROOM: ....

SUBJECT:...

TEACHER:..

EMAIL:...

ROOM:...

SUBJECT:...

TEACHER:..

EMAIL:...

ROOM:...

SUBJECT:...

TEACHER:..

EMAIL:...

ROOM:...

SUBJECT:...

TEACHER:..

EMAIL:...

ROOM:...

August ♡

Thursday

Friday

Saturday

TO-DO

TO-DO

Sunday

We go together like
milk & cookies

Monday

16

Today going
To go
To

NJ
new jersey

TO-DO

Tuesday

17

I
made
A
Song

TO-DO

Wednesday

18

going
Back
To

MaSS w/friends

TO-DO

This might be the Mondayest
Wednesday ever!

Thursday

19

Nothing

Friday

20

Nothing

Saturday

Sunday

TO-DO

TO-DO

NOTES

Monday

Tuesday

Wednesday

TO-DO

TO-DO

TO-DO

NOTES

Thursday

Friday

Saturday

TO-DO

TO-DO

Sunday

Every plan starts without a plan

Monday	Tuesday	Wednesday

TO-DO	TO-DO	TO-DO

When nothing is sure,
everything is possible

MARGARETH DABBLE

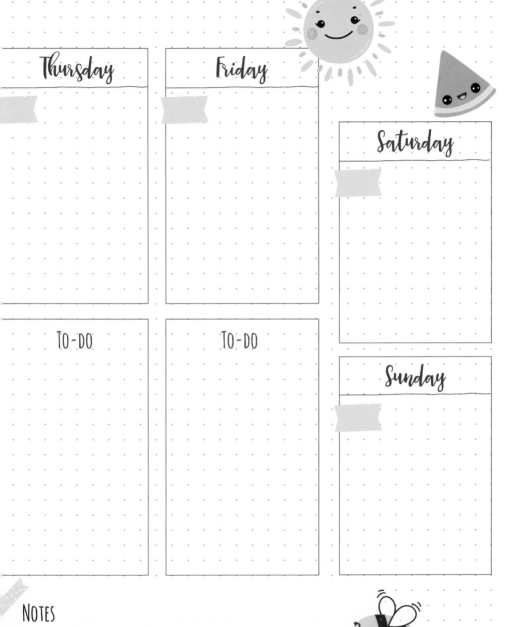

Thursday

Friday

Saturday

TO-DO

TO-DO

Sunday

NOTES

Box-Sets

Create a wishlist for any series you want to watch
and then give them a star rating once you have.

○ The mandalorian ⭐️☆☆☆☆

○ _____ ☆☆☆☆☆

○ _____ ☆☆☆☆☆

○ _____ ☆☆☆☆☆

○ _____ ☆☆☆☆☆

○ _____ ☆☆☆☆☆

○ _____ ☆☆☆☆☆

○ _____ ☆☆☆☆☆

○ _____ ☆☆☆☆☆

○ _____ ☆☆☆☆☆

○ _____ ☆☆☆☆☆

○ _____ ☆☆☆☆☆

○ _____ ☆☆☆☆☆

○ _____ ☆☆☆☆☆

○ _____ ☆☆☆☆☆

○ _____ ☆☆☆☆☆

○ _____ ☆☆☆☆☆

September

1
2
3
4
5
6
7
8
9
10
11
12
13
14
15
16
17
18
19
20
21
22
23
24
25
26
27
28
29
30
31

Monday

Tuesday

Wednesday

TO-DO

TO-DO

TO-DO

NOTES

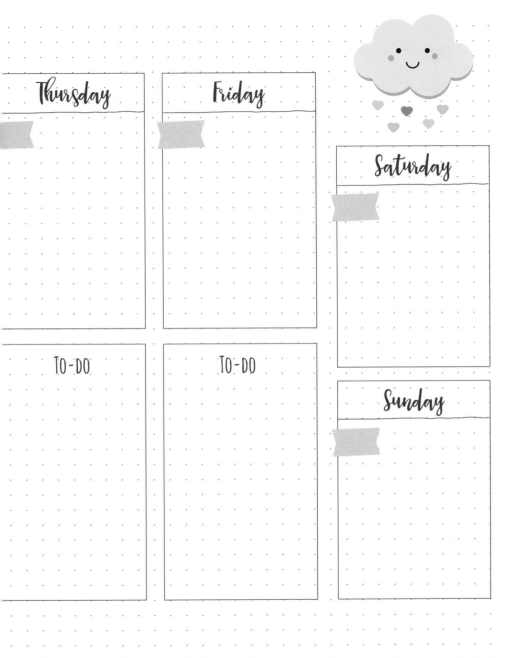

Thursday

Friday

Saturday

TO-DO

TO-DO

Sunday

Be a warrior not a worrier

Monday

Tuesday

Wednesday

TO-DO

TO-DO

TO-DO

NOTES

Thursday

Friday

Saturday

TO-DO

TO-DO

Sunday

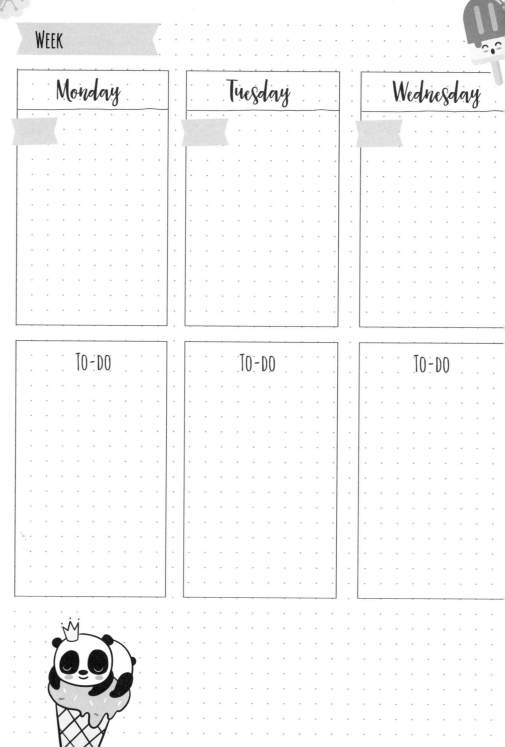

WEEK

Monday

Tuesday

Wednesday

TO-DO

TO-DO

TO-DO

Thursday

Friday

Saturday

TO-DO

TO-DO

Sunday

NOTES

Monday

Tuesday

Wednesday

TO-DO

TO-DO

TO-DO

NOTES

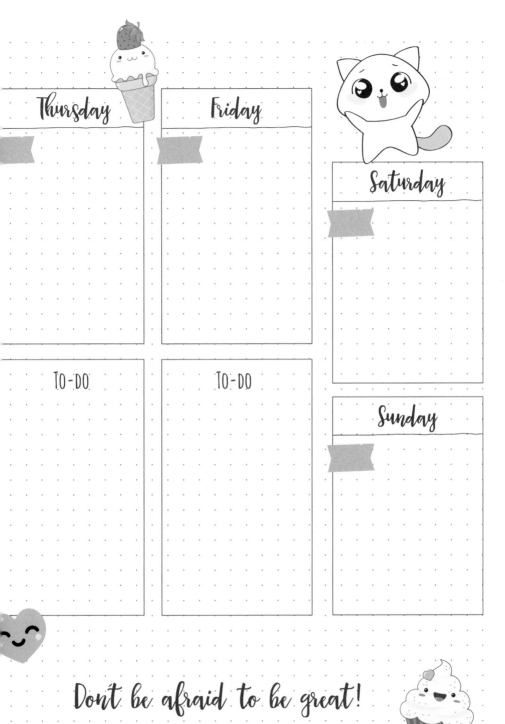

Thursday

Friday

Saturday

TO-DO

TO-DO

Sunday

Don't be afraid to be great!

Notes

What's on your mind? Doodle it here!

Monthly Overview

1 ....

2 ....

3 ....

4 ....

5 ....

6 ....

7 ....

8 ....

9 ....

10 ....

11 ....

12 ....

13 ....

14 ....

15 ....

16 ....

17 ....

18 ....

19 ....

20 ....

21 ....

22 ....

23 ....

24 ....

25 ....

26 ....

27 ....

28 ....

29 ....

30 ....

31 ....

Monday

Tuesday

Wednesday

To-Do

To-Do

To-Do

We all have to think so why not think positive?

Thursday

Friday

Saturday

TO-DO

TO-DO

Sunday

NOTES

WEEK

Monday

Tuesday

Wednesday

TO-DO

TO-DO

TO-DO

NOTES

44

Thursday

Friday

Saturday

TO-DO

TO-DO

Sunday

Sometimes we're so quick to count the days
that we forget to make the days count

Monday

TO-DO

Tuesday

TO-DO

Wednesday

TO-DO

NOTES

Thursday

Friday

Saturday

TO-DO

TO-DO

Sunday

Create your own sunshine

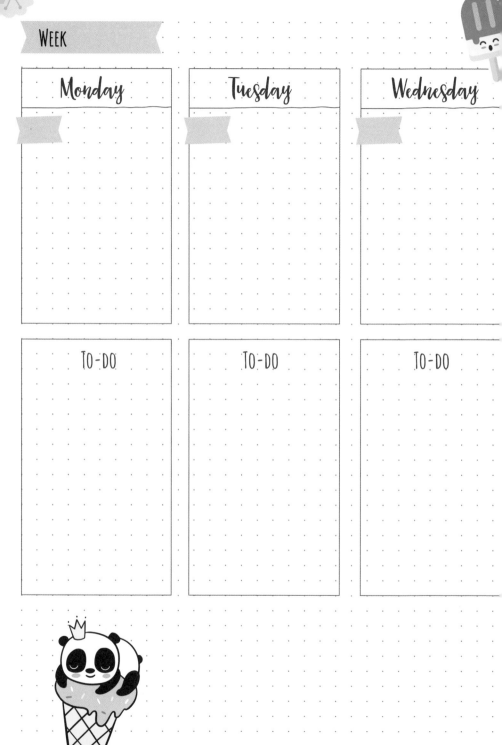

Week

Monday

Tuesday

Wednesday

To-Do

To-Do

To-Do

Thursday

Friday

Saturday

To-Do

To-Do

Sunday

NOTES

My Bucket List: BFF-Edition

Experience new adventures! You've probably already planned lots of great things to do with your friends. Write them down here so you don't forget them!

- ○ _____
- ○ _____
- ○ _____
- ○ _____
- ○ _____
- ○ _____
- ○ _____
- ○ _____
- ○ _____
- ○ _____
- ○ _____
- ○ _____
- ○ _____
- ○ _____
- ○ _____
- ○ _____

Must-Haves

When you have no money, you can think of loads of things you'd like, but then when the time comes you can't remember any of them! If this sounds familiar, why not write down all your shopping wants here?

MUST-HAVE	PURPOSE	PRICE	BOUGHT!

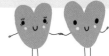

1
2
3
4
5
6
7
8
9
10
11
12
13
14
15
16
17
18
19
20
21
22
23
24
25
26
27
28
29
30
31

Monday

Tuesday

Wednesday

To-Do

To-Do

To-Do

Notes

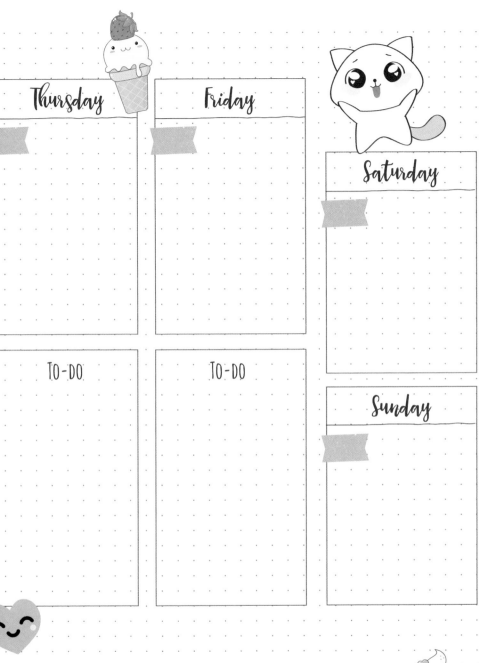

Thursday

Friday

Saturday

TO-DO

TO-DO

Sunday

Creativity is intelligence having fun

ALBERT EINSTEIN

Monday

Tuesday

Wednesday

TO-DO

TO-DO

TO-DO

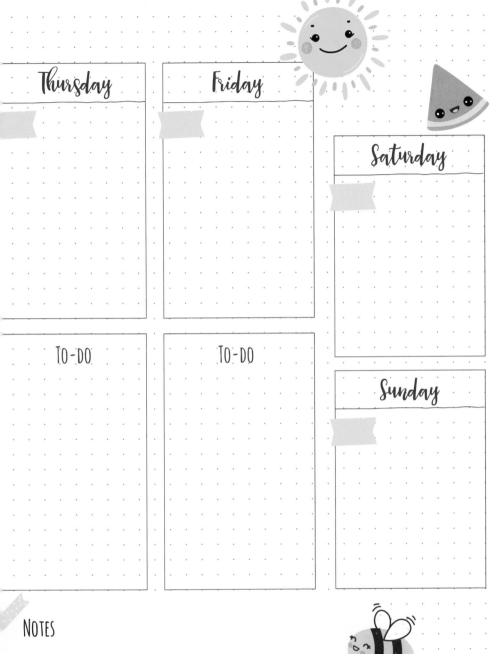

Thursday

Friday

Saturday

To-do

To-do

Sunday

Notes

Monday

Tuesday

Wednesday

TO-DO

TO-DO

TO-DO

NOTES

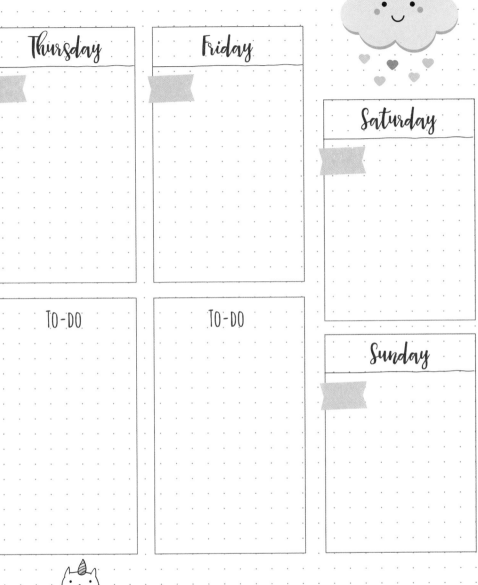

Thursday

Friday

Saturday

TO-DO

TO-DO

Sunday

Some days you just have to create your own sunshine

WEEK

Monday

Tuesday

Wednesday

TO-DO

TO-DO

TO-DO

NOTES

Thursday

Friday

Saturday

TO-DO

TO-DO

Sunday

Follow your dreams,
they know the way

My Bucket List

On this bucket list you can record what you really want
to do this summer. By writing your ideas down here, you
won't forget them and your summer won't be boring!

- ○
- ○
- ○
- ○
- ○
- ○
- ○
- ○
- ○
- ○
- ○
- ○
- ○
- ○
- ○
- ○
- ○

Are there things you really want to do in the next
few years? What dreams do you want to fulfil?
Write them down here and then tick them off!

- ○ TRy And Be That Girl!
- ○ ~~Get Hight~~ Get High grades in 6th grade
- ○
- ○
- ○
- ○
- ○
- ○
- ○
- ○
- ○
- ○
- ○
- ○
- ○
- ○
- ○

Monthly Overview

1
2
3
4
5
6
7
8
9
10
11
12
13
14
15
16
17
18
19
20
21
22
23
24
25
26
27
28
29
30
31

Monday

Tuesday

Wednesday

To-Do

To-Do

To-Do

Thinking is difficult, that's why most people judge

— CARL JUNG

Thursday

Friday

Saturday

To-Do

To-Do

Sunday

Notes

Monday

Tuesday

Wednesday

TO-DO

TO-DO

TO-DO

NOTES

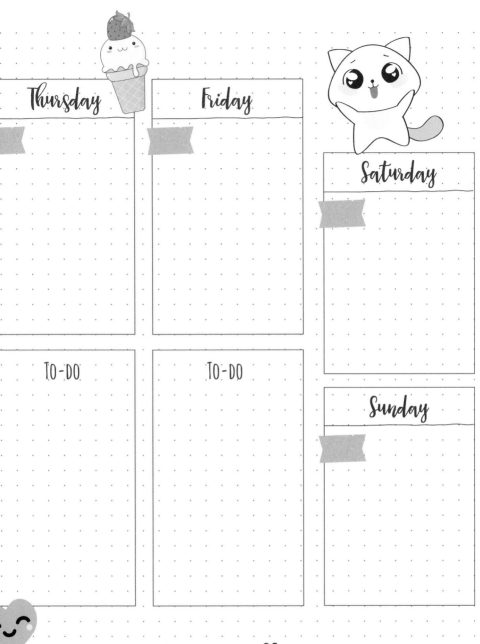

Thursday

Friday

Saturday

TO-DO

TO-DO

Sunday

Be yourself.
Everyone else already exists

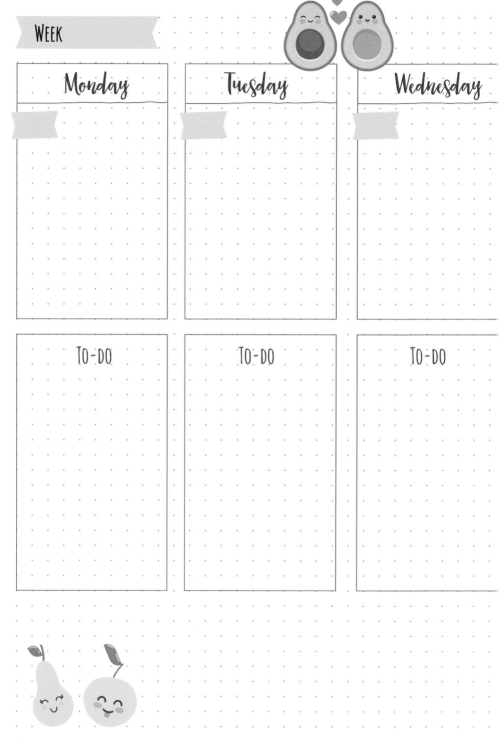

Week

Monday

Tuesday

Wednesday

To-do

To-do

To-do

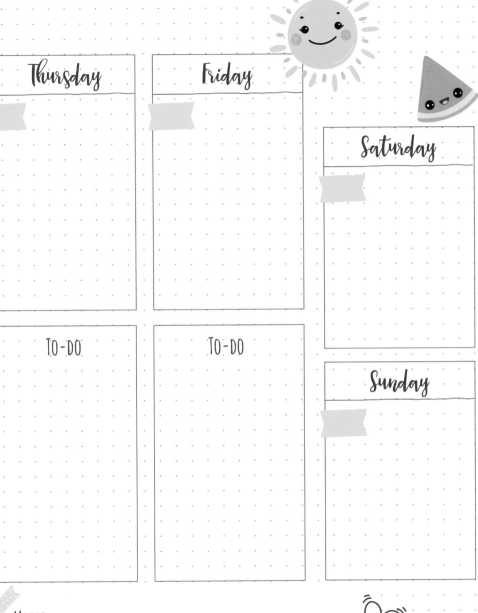

Thursday

Friday

Saturday

Sunday

TO-DO

TO-DO

NOTES

Monday

Tuesday

Wednesday

TO-DO

TO-DO

TO-DO

NOTES

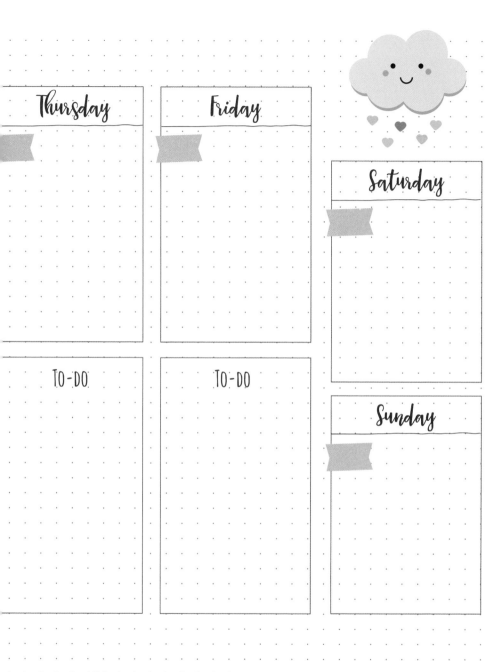

Thursday

Friday

Saturday

Sunday

TO-DO

TO-DO

Old ways won't open new doors

Cool DIY Projects

Make a list of things you want to make: it could be
recipes, craft projects or upcycling ideas... go!

Loaned and Borrowed

Keep track of all the things you have either
loaned to friends or borrowed yourself.

Object	Borrowed	Loaned	To/From	Returned

Always lend a helping hand

Monthly Overview

1
2
3
4
5
6
7
8
9
10
11
12
13
14
15
16
17
18
19
20
21
22
23
24
25
26
27
28
29
30
31

Monday

Tuesday

Wednesday

TO-DO

TO-DO

TO-DO

NOTES

Thursday

Friday

Saturday

TO-DO

TO-DO

Sunday

Donut Worry, be Happy!

Monday

TO-DO

Tuesday

TO-DO

Wednesday

TO-DO

Go outside and
get some sunshine

Thursday

Friday

Saturday

TO-DO

TO-DO

Sunday

NOTES

Monday

Tuesday

Wednesday

TO-DO

TO-DO

TO-DO

NOTES

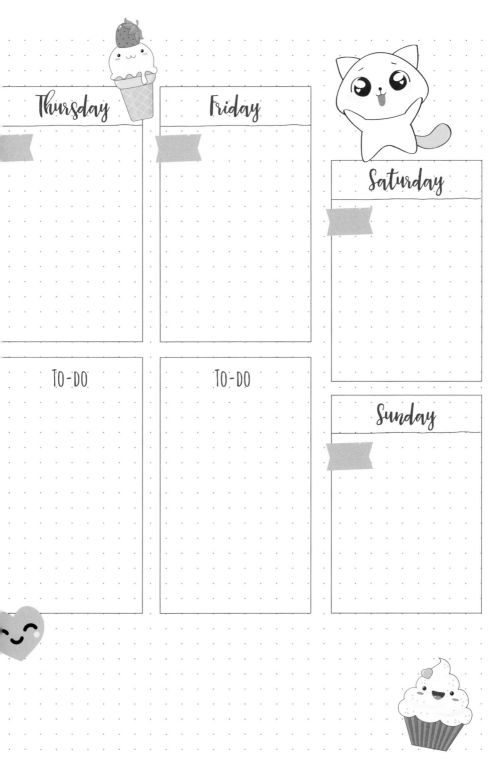

Thursday

Friday

Saturday

TO-DO

TO-DO

Sunday

Monday

Tuesday

Wednesday

TO-DO

TO-DO

TO-DO

It's Friday... time to make stories for Monday!

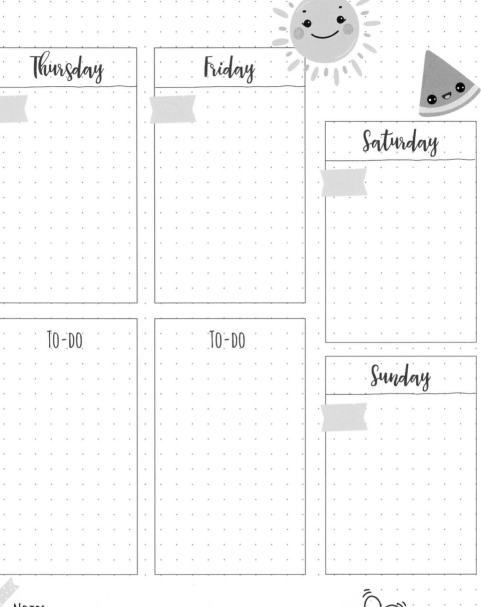

Thursday

Friday

Saturday

TO-DO

TO-DO

Sunday

NOTES

My Books

Which books do you really want to read?

○ _____

○ _____

○ _____

○ _____

○ _____

○ _____

○ _____

○ _____

○ _____

○ _____

○ _____

○ _____

○ _____

○ _____

○ _____

○ _____

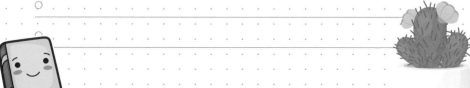

My Travels

Where do you want to visit?

- Australia
- Paris
- Rio
- Alaska
- greenland
- icelanad
-
-
-
-
-
-
-
-
-
-

Monthly Overview

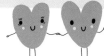

1
2
3
4
5
6
7
8
9
10
11
12
13
14
15
16
17
18
19
20
21
22
23
24
25
26
27
28
29
30
31

Monday

Tuesday

Wednesday

TO-DO

TO-DO

TO-DO

NOTES

Thursday

Friday

Saturday

TO-DO

TO-DO

Sunday

Let's explore this awesome world

Monday

Tuesday

Wednesday

TO-DO

TO-DO

TO-DO

NOTES

Thursday

Friday

Saturday

TO-DO

TO-DO

Sunday

Coffee in one hand,
confidence in the other

Monday

Tuesday

Wednesday

TO-DO

TO-DO

TO-DO

Thursday

Friday

Saturday

TO-DO

TO-DO

Sunday

NOTES

Monday

Tuesday

Wednesday

To-Do

To-Do

To-Do

NOTES

Thursday

Friday

Saturday

TO-DO

TO-DO

Sunday

Every day is a fresh start

Let's Play!

Banish boredom here! Why not play tic-tac-toe, hangman or battleships?

1
2
3
4
5
6
7
8
9
10
11
12
13
14
15
16
17
18
19
20
21
22
23
24
25
26
27
28
29
30
31

Monday

Tuesday

Wednesday

TO-DO

TO-DO

TO-DO

Thursday

Friday

Saturday

To-do

To-do

Sunday

NOTES

Monday

Tuesday

Wednesday

TO-DO

TO-DO

TO-DO

NOTES

Thursday

Friday

Saturday

TO-DO

TO-DO

Sunday

Life is art - live yours in colour

Monday

Tuesday

Wednesday

To-Do

To-Do

To-Do

Notes

Thursday

Friday

Saturday

Sunday

TO-DO

TO-DO

Week

Monday

Tuesday

Wednesday

To-Do

To-Do

To-Do

She had the soul of a gypsy, the heart of a hippie and the spirit of a fairy

Thursday

Friday

Saturday

TO-DO

TO-DO

Sunday

NOTES

Social Media

Plan your next posts or write down ideas!

Inspiration

Write down quotes and sayings
that you particularly like!

○ _____

○ _____

○ _____

○ _____

○ _____

○ _____

○ _____

○ _____

○ _____

○ _____

○ _____

○ _____

○ _____

○ _____

*To be irreplaceable, you
have to be different*

COCO CHANEL

1
2
3
4
5
6
7
8
9
10
11
12
13
14
15
16
17
18
19
20
21
22
23
24
25
26
27
28
29
30
31

Monday

Tuesday

Wednesday

To-do

To-do

To-do

Notes

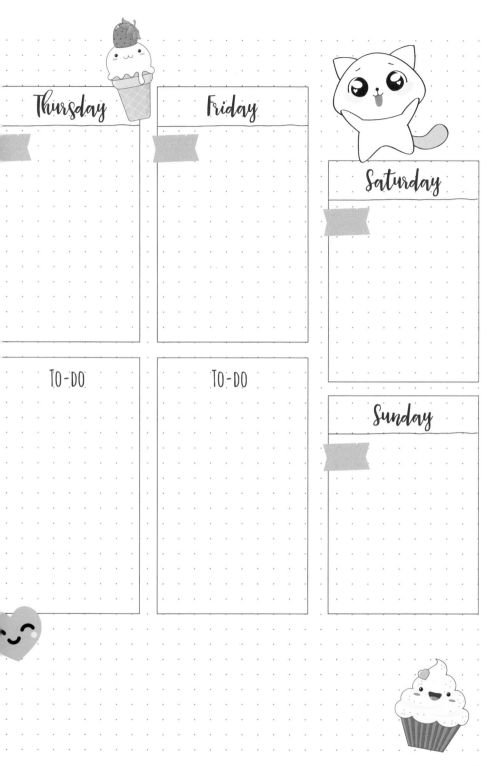

Thursday

Friday

Saturday

Sunday

TO-DO

TO-DO

Monday

TO-DO

Tuesday

TO-DO

Wednesday

TO-DO

It is what it is but it will be what you make of it!

Thursday

Friday

Saturday

TO-DO

TO-DO

Sunday

NOTES

Monday

Tuesday

Wednesday

TO-DO

TO-DO

TO-DO

NOTES

Thursday

Friday

Saturday

TO-DO

TO-DO

Sunday

Enjoy the little things

Monday

Tuesday

Wednesday

To-do

To-do

To-do

Notes

Thursday

Friday

Saturday

TO-DO

TO-DO

Sunday

Donut be afraid to make mistakes

Make a list of the films you want to watch
and then give them a star rating once you have.

- ☆☆☆☆☆
- ☆☆☆☆☆
- ☆☆☆☆☆
- ☆☆☆☆☆
- ☆☆☆☆☆
- ☆☆☆☆☆
- ☆☆☆☆☆
- ☆☆☆☆☆
- ☆☆☆☆☆
- ☆☆☆☆☆
- ☆☆☆☆☆
- ☆☆☆☆☆
- ☆☆☆☆☆
- ☆☆☆☆☆
- ☆☆☆☆☆
- ☆☆☆☆☆
- ☆☆☆☆☆
- ☆☆☆☆☆

Notes

1

2

3

4

5

6

7

8

9

10

11

12

13

14

15

16

17

18

19

20

21

22

23

24

25

26

27

28

29

30

31

Monday

TO-DO

Tuesday

TO-DO

Wednesday

TO-DO

Storms give trees deeper roots

Thursday

Friday

Saturday

To-do

To-do

Sunday

Notes

Monday

Tuesday

Wednesday

To-do

To-do

To-do

NOTES

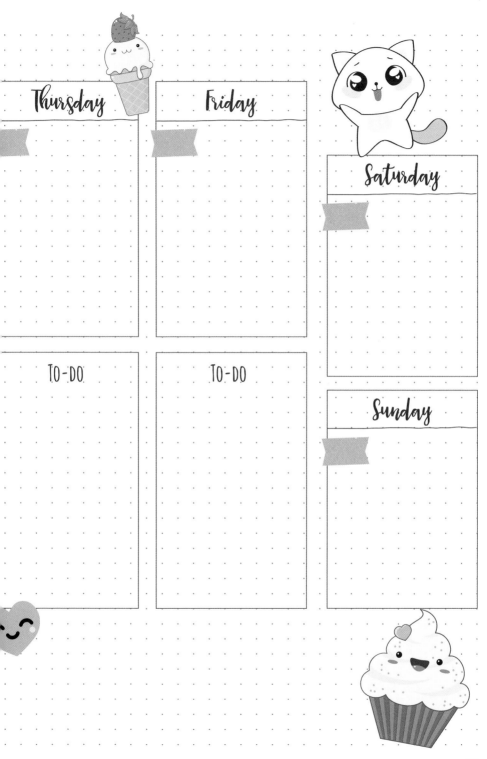

Thursday

Friday

Saturday

TO-DO

TO-DO

Sunday

Monday

Tuesday

Wednesday

To-do

To-do

To-do

Thursday

Friday

Saturday

To-do

To-do

Sunday

Notes

Monday

Tuesday

Wednesday

TO-DO

TO-DO

TO-DO

NOTES

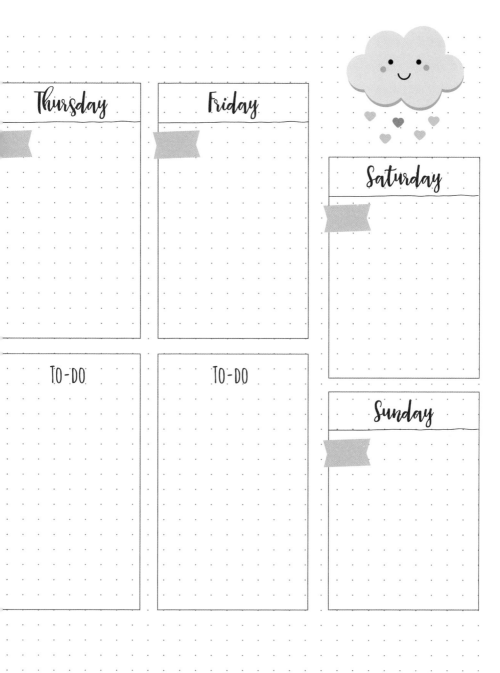

Thursday

Friday

Saturday

Sunday

TO-DO

TO-DO

I need Google in my brain

Money Tracker

Keep track of all your expenses and income. If you want to get an exact picture for each month, simply copy this table for each month onto a new sheet of paper.

Budget

Income	Expenses	Purpose

INCOME	EXPENSES	PURPOSE

1
2
3
4
5
6
7
8
9
10
11
12
13
14
15
16
17
18
19
20
21
22
23
24
25
26
27
28
29
30
31

Monday

Tuesday

Wednesday

TO-DO

TO-DO

TO-DO

NOTES

Thursday

Friday

Saturday

TO-DO

TO-DO

Sunday

What a cute-tea!

Monday

Tuesday

Wednesday

TO-DO

TO-DO

TO-DO

Laughter is the best medicine

Thursday

Friday

Saturday

TO-DO

TO-DO

Sunday

NOTES

Monday

Tuesday

Wednesday

TO-DO

TO-DO

TO-DO

NOTES

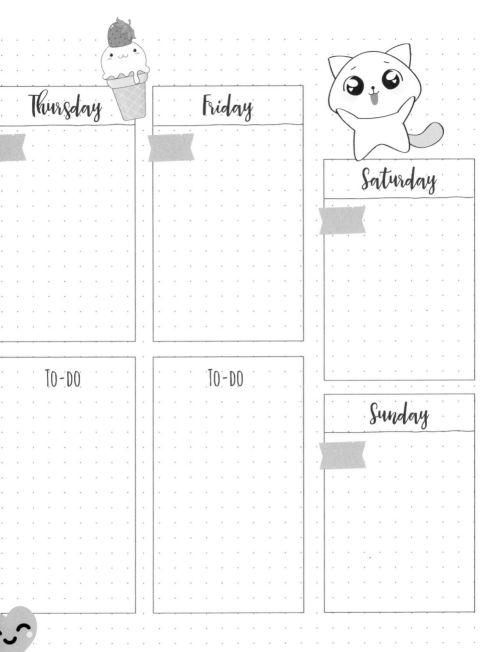

Thursday

Friday

TO-DO

TO-DO

Saturday

Sunday

If you don't understand,
just nod and smile!

Monday

Tuesday

Wednesday

TO-DO

TO-DO

TO-DO

1+1=2

Just because the solution is easy doesn't mean it is wrong

Thursday

Friday

Saturday

TO-DO

TO-DO

Sunday

NOTES

Monthly Overview

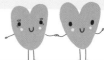

1
2
3
4
5
6
7
8
9
10
11
12
13
14
15
16
17
18
19
20
21
22
23
24
25
26
27
28
29
30
31

Monday

Tuesday

Wednesday

To-do

To-do

To-do

NOTES

Thursday

Friday

Saturday

TO-DO

TO-DO

Sunday

Hoping for change without doing something
is like waiting for a ship at the station

Monday

Tuesday

Wednesday

TO-DO

TO-DO

TO-DO

NOTES

Thursday

Friday

Saturday

TO-DO

TO-DO

Sunday

I love you so matcha

Monday

To-do

Tuesday

To-do

Wednesday

To-do

When someone says:
'that's impossible', remember these
are their limits, not yours

Thursday

Friday

Saturday

To-do

To-do

Sunday

NOTES

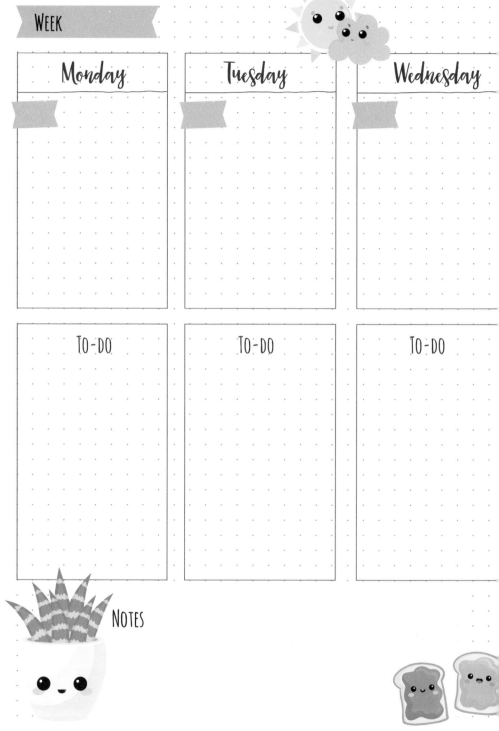

Monday

Tuesday

Wednesday

To-do

To-do

To-do

Notes

Thursday

Friday

Saturday

TO-DO

TO-DO

Sunday

Live life to the fullest every day

Learning Plan

Here's a template to help you prepare for tests and plan for exams. More exams? Copy it onto more sheets!

Subject:...

Test/exam date:................................

Study Set	Need to Learn	Learning	Learned

Subject:...

Test/exam date:................................

Study Set	Need to Learn	Learning	Learned

Subject:..

Test/exam date:...

Study Set	Need to Learn	Learning	Learned

Subject:..

Test/exam date:...

Study Set	Need to Learn	Learning	Learned

Monthly Overview

1

2

3

4

5

6

7

8

9

10

11

12

13

14

15

16

17

18

19

20

21

22

23

24

25

26

27

28

29

30

31

Monday

Tuesday

Wednesday

TO-DO

TO-DO

TO-DO

A goal without a plan
is just a wish

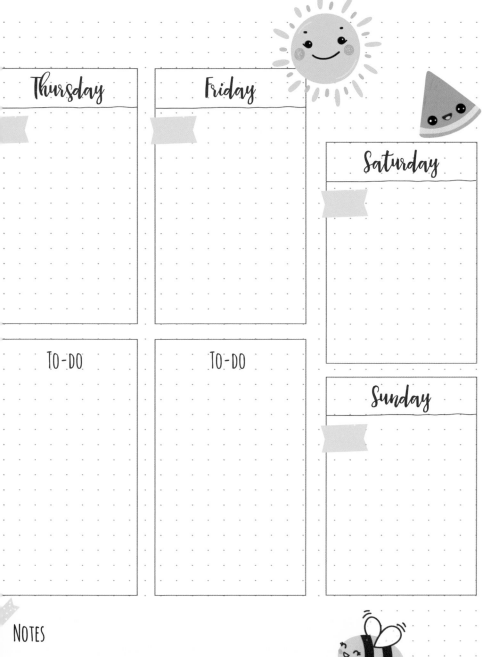

Thursday

Friday

Saturday

TO-DO

TO-DO

Sunday

NOTES

Monday

Tuesday

Wednesday

TO-DO

TO-DO

TO-DO

NOTES

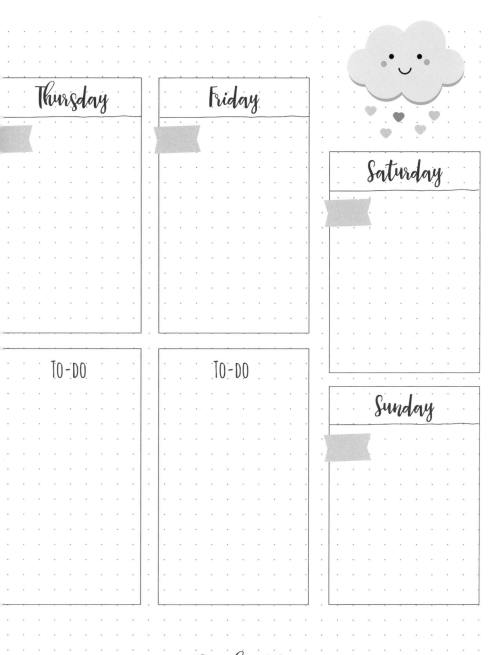

Thursday

Friday

Saturday

Sunday

TO-DO

TO-DO

You can't take the lift to success.
You have to take the stairs

Monday

Tuesday

Wednesday

To-do

To-do

To-do

Notes

Thursday

Friday

Saturday

TO-DO

TO-DO

Sunday

Monday

TO-DO

Tuesday

TO-DO

Wednesday

TO-DO

If travelling were free,
you'd never see me again

Thursday

Friday

Saturday

TO-DO

TO-DO

Sunday

NOTES

Monday

Tuesday

Wednesday

To-do

To-do

To-do

Notes

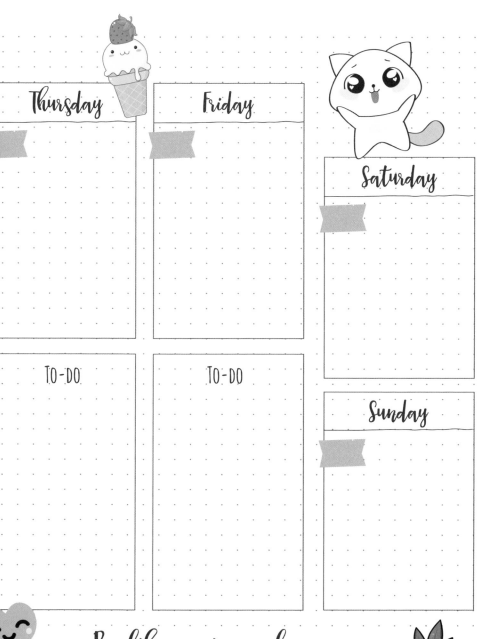

Thursday

Friday

Saturday

TO-DO

TO-DO

Sunday

Be like a pineapple -
stand up straight, wear a crown
and be sweet on the inside!

My Wishlist

Record your birthday and
Christmas wishes here!

○ _____

○ _____

○ _____

○ _____

○ _____

○ _____

○ _____

○ _____

○ _____

○ _____

○ _____

○ _____

○ _____

○ _____

○ _____

○ _____

Gift Ideas

Do you have gift ideas for your best friend, parents or siblings? Write them down here so you don't forget them!

GIFT	FOR

Highlights

Write down the funniest and most beautiful moments of the year here so you will never forget them!

Mood Tracker

Track your daily mood for a whole month! Here are templates for two months. If you'd like to follow your mood every month, just copy the star garlands onto a new sheet of paper! A star represents a day. Set a colour for each mood and shade the stars in the right colour every day.

A DAVID AND CHARLES BOOK
© Edition Michael Fischer GmbH, 2020
www.emf-verlag.de

David and Charles is an imprint of David and Charles, Ltd
1 Emperor Way, Exeter Business Park, Exeter, EX1 3QS

This translation of MY KAWAII JOURNAL first published in Germany by Edition Michael Fischer GmbH in
2020 is published by arrangement with Silke Bruenink Agency, Munich, Germany.

First published in the UK and USA in 2020

All rights reserved. No part of this publication may be reproduced in any form or by any means, electronic or
mechanical, by photocopying, recording or otherwise, without prior permission in writing from the publisher.

A catalogue record for this book is available from the British Library.
ISBN-13: 9781446308462 paperback

Printed by Polygraf in the Slovak Republic for:
David and Charles, Ltd
1 Emperor Way, Exeter Business Park, Exeter, EX1 3QS

10 9 8 7 6 5 4 3 2 1

Cover design and typesetting: Bernadett Linseisen
Layout: Meritt Hettwer, Bernadett Linseisen
Text: Mareike Schlesog, Greta Ruppaner, Marcelina Schulte
Product management: Marcelina Schulte
Image credits: © Incomible/Shutterstock, © RedKoala/Shutterstock, © MaryMo/Shutterstock, © ayelet-
keshet/Shutterstock, © Cute little things/Shutterstock, © Nataliya Dolotko/Shutterstock, © teamplay/
Shutterstock, © Shannon Marie Ferguson/Shutterstock, © Anna Kutukova/Shutterstock, © Jinpat/Shutter-
stock, © Aleksey Zhuravlev/Shutterstock, © Margarita_V/Shutterstock, © Viaire/Shutterstock, © Caupona/
Shutterstock, © antinov/Shutterstock, © ksuklein/Shutterstock, © Studio_G/Shutterstock, © Jemastock/
Shutterstock, © zizi_mentos/Shutterstock, © Poppy_Field/Shutterstock, © Bibadash/Shutterstock, © Hap-
pypictures/Shutterstock, © April_pie/Shutterstock, © Maria Skrigan/Shutterstock, © gst/Shutterstock,
© Lukiyanova Natalia frenta/Shutterstock, © Marianna Pashchuk/Shutterstock, © Panuwach/Shutterstock,
© Ekaterina Chvileva/Shutterstock, © Nadezda Barkova/Shutterstock, © lena_nikolaeva/Shutterstock,
© yopinco/Shutterstock, © Roi and Roi/Shutterstock, © anna1195/Shutterstock, © CraftCloud/Shutter-
stock, © YourElechka/Shutterstock, © Snejana111/Shutterstock, © USBFCO/Shutterstock, © Shade-
Design/Shutterstock, © mhatzapa/Shutterstock, © AllNikArt/Shutterstock, © suniwa/Shutterstock,
© Olga Kashubin/Shutterstock.

David and Charles publishes high-quality books on a wide range of subjects.
For more information visit www.davidandcharles.com.